Tactical Magic

Tactical Magic

A fieldbook for the professional mage

Aaron M. McKagantry

COVENSTEAD PRESS　　　BUFFALO, NEW YORK

Contents

Introduction

Wiccans, Witches, Pagans, Diabolists, Metaphysicists, shamans and mystics usually vary in their individual usage of or experiences with magic. Most only use it for personal and religious needs, or to engage in local power struggles that go way over the heads of those uninvolved in magic. You can call these people mundanes, or muggles, or cowans, but those of us who practice true tactical magic simply call them *civilians.*

Civilians usually don't care about the rest of us, but they call upon us nonetheless, usually for reasons that we *know* are stupid. They think they've been cursed, they think that the Ouija board they were sold has demons in it, they think their house is haunted. As a result of this generally misguided nonsense, many of us spend precious time on them when we could be doing important things like raising our families and passing exams.

This is book is for any mage that has ever gotten a C instead of an A because s/he was standing in a graveyard at three in the morning appeasing an angry ghost at the behest of a client who just called and sobbed that his or her life was *over* if nothing was done to stop the madness. It is for anyone who has ever prayed for an open gas station on a dark country road because someone's child had tried Diabolism for Dummies and Mom and Dad couldn't sleep in a tainted house. It's for everyone who has ever battled dragons, faeries or elves to make it better for some distraught dabbler who got in over their head and became scared.

This book will teach you how to spot a changeling or the reincarnation of King Arthur or a child born with special powers. Statistically, every child you will have brought to you will be normal, every Ouija board a cheap game and every ghost just a hint of hysteria. With TV shows and the like making magic romantic, and witch "schools" making everyone who can afford to pay into a "certified Witch," your knowledge, even if it's very small, makes you an expert compared to civilians.

Whether your path is from the Right Hand, the Left or somewhere in between, we all know that when civilians get hysterical *everyone* suffers. If the freaky tenant in your building starts screaming that the darkside is hovering in the hallway, the landlord is going to ask the innocent Pagan or Mage to leave to make her feel better. That you had *nothing* to do with it means nothing, you're going to find yourself evicted, and while you'd win in court, statistically you can't afford the lawyer you need to get there.

If you can learn instead to place the crazy lady's fears at ease, you can avoid all the nonsense in the first place. This is what tactical magic is, it is the use of minor metaphysics to convince civilians to go their own way and leave us to our own worlds of magic in peace. This book will teach you how to get left alone by the civilians and the wannabes, regardless of your levels of power or training. You will become a supreme tactician of magic, able to beat off anything they send up against you.

Civilians and Talent

C ivilians are not involved with magic for a number of reasons. They don't want to be, they don't believe in magic or they have watched so much television that they think magic is making time stop or teleporting from place to place. None of these people care that mages could demonstrate magic to their heart's content and never have it count as supernatural enough to claim the Randi prize, or that more than ninety percent of what a mage does is about the inner journey and affecting change inside the mage and inside his will. Civilians are invested in worlds of feeling and experience, moving from emotional highs to emotional lows with no understanding of what goes on.

Civilization enforces this. In the past, you worked the fields or a trade until you were exhausted; today you need to work an ungodly number of hours to afford a comfortable lifestyle. By keeping people tired and poor, cultures create a second class citizenry of people who can be led by their emotions and animal drives. A politician need only talk about fear and sex to get their vote because voters haven't the opportunity to seriously think about what they believe. Civilians are time deprived, having to go from sleep to work to food to sleep to work once more, literally having no time to think.

Unfortunately, the skillset required to perceive magic is not limited to the people who either have time to think or know to make time to think. People with too little training and just a little too much interest perceive energies and forces around them, the play of emotions and morals, the energy of civilization. Most of them sensibly dismiss these energies and go about their business, but some of them take these hunches and perceptions to a place of hysteria and maladaptive nonsense.

Worse, many of them have one or two experiences of a metaphysical nature as a child, when they are most suggestible and then decide that an emotional state is the same as a metaphysical experience.

The example of the crazy lady in the apartment building actually happened to a friend of mine. There was an exceedingly ill-behaved Charismatic Christian follower living in his building, and it was certain that she had some small skill in picking up the emotions of other people, no matter how well hidden. People who accepted her were "of the light" and people who disliked her, or disagreed with her were the agents of Satan.

This is a reoccurring pattern in some Charismatic Christians, who are literally taught that Satan is hiding around the corner, ready to leap out and say "boo!" As a result, they take *any* sensation that is not of the normal kind and assume it is Satan. In my friend's building there had been a domestic dispute, and a woman was shot on the stairwell. This place had a palpable feeling of pain to it, mostly because the woman had lived and most of the people in the building knew her, and knew where she'd been shot. The paint in this spot was new, as was some of the molding, and it was very clearly set apart as different.... Which any mage should realize made the energies of the space different and would've done so even without the domestic dispute.

This hysterical Christian decided this stairwell corner had the feeling of Satan to it, and hired ghost hunters, also civilians, to "investigate" the corner. They claimed, of course, that the area had "deep cosmic energy" or some such nonsense and she took this to mean that satanic energies were present. This is a common phenomenon with civilians, in that if one claims the energies of a place comes from UFOs, and another claims the energies come from an Indian burial ground and a third claims the feelings come from faeries, they all take each other's "proof" as proof of their particular theory.

The hapless mage living on the same floor as the infamous stairwell saw the direction this was going and first tried to talk to the ghost hunters and then to the Charismatic Christian. When at last he realized he was going to get nowhere with this, he convinced the super to let him perform a simple banishing ritual on the area to get rid of the "satanic energy." He also agreed to paint the *other* stairwells of the building, feeding the super some nonsense about this disrupting the darkness.

The super was of the opinion they were all nuts, but the mage in question *was* a professional painter, and he'd agreed to do the other stairwells for free, so he conceded. The mage had one more trick up his sleeve, convincing the woman who had been shot that it was vital that she help him get rid of the ghost hunters, who'd decided the building was interesting and were now trying to get the super to allow them to shoot footage for some television show.

Like a good mage, he always had another ace up his sleeve, so he talked to a Catholic priest in his neighborhood and explained the situation, discussing the fact that he sincerely feared for the mental health of the Christian lady. He arranged for the building to be blessed by the priest, and also explained to the non-Christians in the building why this was happening. Remember that this Charismatic Christian lady was not very stable, and keeping her content was something *everyone* in the building felt invested in, so even the non-Christians agreed that setting her at ease was good for everyone.

While she watched, our mage performed a basic banishing and purification rite, which was recognizable to this woman as Abrahamic in origin, and thus made her feel more comfortable. Since she had *just enough* talent to feel that *something* was going on, but not enough talent to understand her own emotions, she felt that something tangible and real had been done.

The repainting and the blessing of the entire building were the next steps, and this calmed the woman, but the ghost hunters were still to be dealt with. If they came in with their pseudoscientific gadgets and "sensed energy" the woman's calm would be dissipated and the nonsense would begin again. As predicted, they "sensed" great terror and angst in the wall at the place on the stairwell where they'd found it before. As arranged, the woman who had been shot insisted that she'd actually been shot one story up, and sure enough, the equipment showed even greater energy upstairs. As discussed, as soon as this happened she acknowledged she was mistaken, and that the incident happened down a flight.

The ghost hunters hemmed and hawed about the energy, but by now it was clear to the woman with the original fears of "satanic energy" that these people didn't know what they were doing and she let her fears die.

Perhaps as much as ninety percent of what mages do for civilians is about showing people with a minor sense of energy that their fears, created by a culture that confuses anything unexplained with magic, are unfounded. To do so, you have to be proactive and demonstrate that other people are yanking their chains.

Most mages want to be left alone, but unless you actively hide, people with the tiniest bit of talent are going to figure out that you know what's going on. *That* is when you can either move on or fix the problem and get on with your life.

When you fix a problem, the magic is the smallest part of it. The largest part is putting the fears of the civilian to rest, and that is ten percent skill, ten percent practice and eighty percent attitude.

A Mage's Attitude

I f you are familiar with the lifestyle of the top two or three mages in history, you know that they were generally extravagant, well read and possessed an attitude that convinced their followers and critics that, regardless of their actual knowledge, they were completely in charge of a situation. If you are familiar with the concept of True Will, you know that if you really, truly, understand and enforce your will, it is an unstoppable force.

Most mages do not know their True Will, and while that is a shame that deserves its own book, it's not something that most civilians really know. If you're one of the millions of mages who does not know your True Will, this chapter will teach you how to *affect* knowledge of your True Will. Remember, with civilians, magic is about appearances and showmanship. They base their views, and their crises, on movies, television shows and fantasy books and if you want to fix their problems, and get on with your life, you need to work within that paradigm.

The first thing you have to do to affect an understanding of your True Will is to be absolutely certain of your abilities. If, for example, a person feels they are possessed, you have to explain to them that you are removing the spirit, but if they still feel the spirit then they have succumbed to a mental delusion as a result of the spirit's influence, and only a psychologist will help. You tell them and believe that your banishment of the spirit is *absolutely definite.* You explain that the *only* way that it will fail is if the disorder is psychological in nature. Certainly as a mage you are aware that the disorder is absolutely psychological in nature, but the civilian's sense of magic will make your banishment feel appropriately strong and help them move on or, hopefully, convince them of their need to get psychological help.

If they've been seen by another mage, or a priest, make it your business to speak to them first. Solidarity amongst metaphysicists is vital to our functioning in a world full of dabbling civilians. Be *very* careful in betraying your hand to your civilian client, who may be the spiritual equivalent of a malingerer, going from mage to mage for help to avoid visiting a shrink or a doctor.

That's not to say you can't tell when someone is a hack and is selling their "magic" to make a buck. You can figure out pretty quickly who is using the paranoia of the sillier civilians to make a living. Most of these people will scurry like cockroaches when the light of a real mage strikes them, but the more vicious ones will not, and those are the ones you should avoid at all costs.

So, assuming you don't know your will, and you're working on it, affecting a True Will can be accomplished by being decisive in your actions, clear and firm in your intentions and absolutely unswayable in your words to the civilians. Remember, always, that they have ideas about magic that are silly and maybe even dangerous to themselves, and if you want to move through the world without their interference, you need to make them feel like when you *do* help them, you're doing it at the expense of your peace and comfort. They've been a terrible bother, so they'll think twice about bothering you in the future...you hope.

There will be those that come to you repeatedly if you let them, bothering you with every creaking branch in a wind storm or bad feeling about a job prospect. You need to draw firm lines before they can get out of hand.

In addition to affecting an understanding of your True Will (or having one), you need to cultivate an air of professionalism. For those of us who are professionals, this is easy, but if you are unemployed, in school or living with your parents you may find that the worst civilians that you come across decide that you operate on their schedule. When I was unemployed, I once drove an hour to help a civilian who claimed to be possessed at 3 in the morning. I made the mistake of not setting clear boundaries with this person because my schedule was wide open.

Don't take "service calls" in the wee hours. In fact, if your phone number gets out there, change it, or have one phone number for the public and one for friends and family. Make yourself unavailable at ridiculous times. People are afraid of the dark; the magic they *need* you for will usually be something they decide they don't need in the daytime. Let them sleep on it.

When you decide to help, help swiftly and decisively. Schedule your appointments and keep them, and dress the part. A mage is supposed to control the powerful forces of the universe, and people, especially civilians, can be terribly concerned about what you look like. You'll need to assess appropriate dress for the occasion, of course. In other words, be as professional as possible. Civilians put a lot of faith in people in suits and uniforms, so use that to your advantage whenever possible.

Remember, always, that civilians have enough magical talent to feel that real magic has occurred, but simultaneously have really, really stupid ideas about magic and the occult. You and I might know that their fears are dumb, but they don't, and if you tell them they are dumb, they'll only decide you're part of the conspiracy too, and then you'll never get any peace!

Ouija Bored

O uija boards constitute about 40% of the nonsense that civilians come up with concerning metaphysics. Although the idea of using a planchette (pointer) or pendulum to point to letters or other characters on a table or slips of paper was common in antiquity, the actual Ouija board as we understand it today was invented in 1890 by two businessmen by the names of Elijah Bond and Charles Kennard, although it would be their employee, William Fuld, who would market the board into the twentieth century. It would be Fuld's board and planchette which would be sold to Parker Brothers in the 1960s and be partially responsible for the nonsense we hear about Ouija boards today.

The board was initially popularized as part of the early twentieth century spiritualism movement, in which the largest entertainment to be found was in attempts to contact the dead. The Ouija board is harmless, of course, but the first critic of the board was Edgar Cayce, who undoubtedly found his own income being threatened by this sort of do-it-yourself contact with the dead. He became the first in a litany of voices against the board, many of whom found their livelihoods threatened by the idea that the common man could be a medium.

There have been cases, very real cases, of mental disorders being severely aggravated by the use of the Ouija board, and almost all of these can be understood as cognitive dissonance or, in extreme cases, schizophrenia and disassociative disorders. Basically, the already fractured civilian uses their own motor control to move the planchette around and then decides the planchette was moved by the dead and spirits. The "advice" from beyond the grave cannot be reconciled with the beliefs of the person and a cognitive breakdown or psychotic break occurs. You can serve as a public mage for a hundred years and never see a single case of Ouija Board hysteria that can't be explained by this phenomenon.

In 1973, the movie The Exorcist featured a brief and somewhat incongruous scene involving a Ouija board which created in many people's heads the idea that the Ouija board was a highway for demons looking for people to possess. Before 1971, when The Exorcist was released in print, civilians didn't get the idea of demons coming into your head from Ouija boards, because the idea is patently stupid—the whole point of the Ouija board is that the spirits that knocked on tables and made cold winds blow could move the planchette with the "energy" that the people touching it gave it. If the planchette moves because a person is moving it (and it does, by the way) then the Ouija board is not working as described.

This may be hard to understand, but basically the demon possession people believe that the Ouija board *works as it claims*, by giving the dead something to move and answer questions, but that this gives the demons a way to get into the bodies of the people using the Ouija board. As you and I know, this is ridiculous. If it's not opening the body to the ghosts, it's certainly not opening the body to demons.

That's not to say there aren't those who believe the mechanism of the Ouija board revolves around channeling, but they are rather few and far between. When dealing with a person convinced the Ouija board has let demons into their house, if you can discover how they think the board works in the first place, this can be an in to their particular psychosis. Always assume psychosis, and always perform magic as if the psychosis is really magical. This will work in all situations, and let the civilian feel that they got what they paid for.

Do not feel any compunction against charging for these rites—all it does is make the civilian feel like you are giving them more. If you can throw a trinket into the deal, more the better for them. If you are a priest, and charging is against your beliefs, you can still tell the client to donate money or time to a cause.

The last rationale you will hear from a civilian regarding Ouija boards, and the one most troubling is that they believe that Ouija boards open portals to the Beyond. They do not. The only thing to do in this scenario is convince the civilian of the error of their assumption, either by convincing them that portals do not exist or by convincing them that Ouija boards work by one of the properties discussed above. You can also try the gate closing technique given later in this work, and explain to them that the Ouija and the gate are unrelated.

Remember at all times that people working with Ouija boards are very suggestible, and you must not make them worse! If you tell them that their problems aren't big and describe a big problem, rest assured that the next time they see you they'll have that big problem!

Purifying Ouija Boards

The easiest purifying technique for the Ouija Board is to use holy water and silk. Holy Water may be obtained from a church, a botanica, a Pagan Priest or Priestess, or, if you have Theurgical skills, by one of the recipes in the materiel section of this work. It's generally best to stick to the faith of your client, as a Christian loony like the neighbor in the first chapter will obviously not be swayed by Pagan holy water, although the "hic, Non expectata vos es" or LBRP will probably work with them.

To purify with silk and holy water, simply asperge the board and wrap it in silk. Make an appropriate prayer of protection, preferably with the client. If they keep the board in the cloth, it will completely shield them from any energies they invoke into the board. Silk, as you no doubt know, has immense shielding properties and is a perfect substrate for holding insulation spells.

You'll have to determine the appropriate level of show for them, but the three by three purification is probably enough for most people.

Three by Three Purification:

While designed for Ouija Boards, specifically, the Three by Three is really effective on other things. It combines real magic, your skills and talents, with showmanship and words that will convince the civilian of the efficacy of your work. You can also inscribe the back of the board with the Three by Three inscription with silver paint, or, if you're doing it outside of your client's view, with a silver paint marker. (Seeing people write with markers seems to make civilians doubt your abilities. I suggest having a desk with a quill and inkpots of silver paint, and maybe even charging for silver ink, followed by a good old indelible silver marker.)

Cast a Circle or use a LBRP to make a space free of outside influence. You should have an altar with charcoal on a censer, holy water in a silver (or gold) container with an asperger or a bundle of herbs for sprinkling the holy water and a red silk cloth for wrapping the board. You'll have to leave the cloth, so make the client pay for it.

The incense should be asafetida or sulfur, but a reasonable replacement is Labdanum. If your client is Christian, Gift of the Magi incense is a reasonable thing to use. Sagebrush is also appropriate. Each of these is less effective than asafetida, but a little more pleasing to work with. Place dampened incense upon charcoal to make a puff of smoke, and draw the board through the smoke. As you do so, spin a basic energy field around the board from your front at heart level, by placing your right hand on the board's front, sliding it up to the outer edge, rotating it and sliding it down the back. When you get to the bottom, turn it over, and press it against your heart, using your will to seal the field. While invisible to the client, this is actually the most important part.

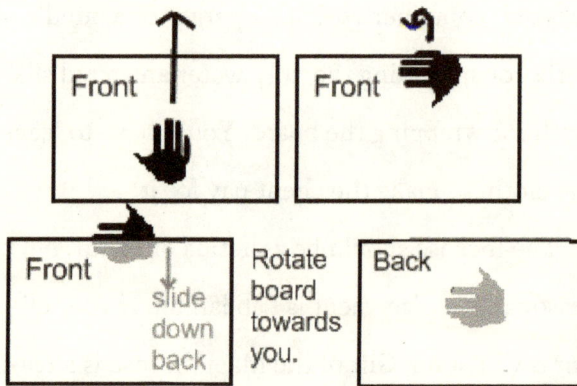

Pull it away from your heart, and pass the board through the smoke again, saying "Spirits, evils, all that see, from this board I demand you flee. Power of air, so must it be, I command thee three by three."

Lay the silk upon the altar, and, with the board facing up, sprinkle it with holy water. Turn it over, doing it again, then once more on its face. "The power of this water[1] compels all who hide within to flee. By the water, so must it be, I command thee, three by three by three."

Fold the cloth inward from the sides, then up from the bottom, then the top down. One line with each fold:

/By the powers of earth I abjure thee/ none may pass save by my will alone/Or with the power of fire I'll render thee/ o ash as cold as frozen stone./

Placing your hand at the center of the covered board, speak the following:

"With the power of air all evil did flee, three by three/With sacred water I bathed thee, three by three by three./ Into an earthen womb, I lay thee, With a promise of flames if thou disobey me/Purified thou now must be. Purified thou now

---

[1] Use the appropriate power for the holy water, obviously.

shall be/As I will so must it be, three by three by three by three.

Instruct the civilian that when they open the cloth to use the last line to remind the board of its obligation of purity. Remind them that unless they will it otherwise, no energies can enter or pass through the board without their explicit permission. Tell them that if they let the energies in intentionally that they should lose your phone number and forget you exist because they will be too stupid to live.

If you must inscribe it, use Theban, thuswise, to say "as I will so mote it be III by III by III by III:"

ᛁᛚ ᛁᛚ ᚱᚱᚢᛋᛋ ᛒᛁᛚ
ᛋᛁᛁᛋᛁᛚ ᚢᛁᛚ ᚨᛁᛚ ᚢᚢᚢ
ᚨᛁᛗ᛬ ᚢᚢᚢ ᚨᛁᛗ᛬ ᚢᚢᚢ
ᚨᛁᛗ᛬ ᚢᚢᚢ

The Three by Three is fun with civilians, because they think it refers to some of the things they have heard on television, but it actually refers to the absence of fire in the ritual. By invoking three elements, you leave the threat of fire hanging. Should you lose control of the purified item, fire will fill the void you've left.

Consecrating Ouija Boards

Instruct the civilian to use a circle, LBRP or centering prayer to cleanse themselves before opening the silk. Once they have opened it, they must take consecrated oil or water and dab it at the corners. They can invoke the angels, elements, elementals, four winds or their gods as you so direct. The purification rite is enough to keep any real energies from getting involved in the process of reading the board, but a civilian isn't going to understand that. Remind them of the very real danger that their board, if used inappropriately, could combust. That seems to keep most of them on the straight and narrow.

When boards go bad...

...or, more accurately, when civilians get stupid.

The following chapters on destroying metaphysical artifacts, closing portals and dealing with possession should cover any stupidity your civilian comes up with regarding an Ouija Board. Remember, the only source of demons or energies in an Ouija Board is the civilian using it. Behave appropriately.

Demolitions Expert

If you're lucky, or insane, you live close enough to a volcano that anytime someone needs a Ouija Board, One Ring or Terminator Robot destroyed you can just chuck them in flaming lava.

Most of us, however, don't live on the slopes of Mount Doom, so the old volcano technique isn't a valid option for us. With that in mind, this chapter deals with destroying things that, for whatever reason, can't just be tossed in the municipal waste, at least can't be tossed in the trash *according to their owners.* These things, such as sacred books, Ouija Boards, enchanted jewelry and the rest, must be destroyed in a way that puts the civilian's mind at rest regarding them.

The first job of a metaphysical demolition expert is to figure out how the item is supposed to work. Jewelry, for the most part, requires integrity to function. Break the jewelry and the spell leaks out, and you, as the mage, should sell the remains to a jeweler for a little extra change. Crystals and glassware can be similarly broken. Books, tarot cards and Ouija boards are powerless in and of themselves and can be burned or recycled.

If an item possesses no innate power and is combustible, it can be burned in a fire pit or a large pot. If it is not combustible, such as a crystal or a piece of metal, and it cannot be shattered, it can be placed in the fastest running water you can find. Find a mage near Niagara Falls, for example, and pay them to toss it off a bridge.

If an item possesses power and does not work on the Principle of Sympathy, transfer the power into a receptacle of your own creation and then destroy it as you would any other powerless object. If your civilian client thinks it is possessed of a curse or a demon, feel free to drain it of power before destroying the object in a manner that appeals to their delusion.

The only very delicate times are when the object works on the Principle of Sympathy. If a client, for example, has a poppet in the form of a friend or enemy, they will often completely believe that the poppet is so strong that even after the spell it was used in has ended, the poppet must be treated delicately or the person will be injured when the poppet is destroyed.

The answer to this is to sever the Sympathetic bond between the object and the person that it represents. To do this, cast a circle, do a LBRP or another rite to clear the area of influence and then invoke the spirit of a deceased person (especially a Right Hand Path Mage!) into the poppet or other item. Call the item by that person's name, and declare that the spell to be cast via the Principle of Sympathy is for that person. Once you have done that, declare that the Poppet or other item looks *nothing like* the deceased person. Declare that this item now represents *Outis*, which was the name Odysseus gave Polyphemus the Cyclops in The Odyssey. Declare that you don't want to do a spell about *Outis*, and break the item down into its components. If sewn, use a seam ripper to open the seams and separate it into its constituents. Burn what can be burned, toss what can't be burned into swift water and bury the ashes. If you have used the name of a deceased person, you may find it best to scatter the ashes at their grave.

I honestly believe that no books are worthless and should therefore be destroyed. If told to destroy a cursed book, I believe that a mage *must* first turn that book into a pdf or otherwise preserve it. Book burners are scary, scary people, and you *don't* want to be a part of that. After all, curses don't fall on ideas or words, but on people and physical objects. A book's contents cannot be cursed, even if a book is. Once you have the contents preserved, burn away.

Transferring power from an object with power into an object without power is very easy. The first step, of course, is to find an object capable of holding power that is also capable of being emptied of power. The easiest objects are non-reflective stones and crystals. If for some reason you are not capable of fully draining an object of power, or you don't like the "feel" of the dregs of power in an object, just pass it on to whatever local mage is good at sucking such things clean. If that's too hard, place it in a super-concentrated solution of salt water and leave it in the "moonlight" from the last quarter to the new moon. Keep it in the dark when not exposed to the moon, and voila, a veritable vampiric vacuum of vacancy will appear....

If you are capable of balancing power in yourself, then you will find it very easy to transfer power from the vessel with power to the vessel without. Holding the empty vessel in your dominant hand, let the energy flow from one side to the other until it reaches an equilibrium. Once it has, you may repeat the procedure with a new empty vessel or use your own techniques to pull power from the vessel you want to empty into the vessel you want to fill. I generally find that two or three empty vessels will be enough to salvage the energy in a charged device without expending any energy.

If I am very lazy, I will simply place three or more empty vessels in a silk lined box with the object to be drained. The natural process of equilibration in the sealed environment is more than enough to drain most objects to the point where disposing of them can occur without worrying about draining them. This is also a good technique for things that are just too yucky to handle.

Simple Fire Disposal Technique for Books, Boards and Cards.

A good demolition should invoke the power of each of the elements, since most mages have some form of belief in the elements, whether in a CM "archangel" understanding or a more Hellenic/Pagan understanding. Use an 80% alcohol mixture in your water, and pass it through water, through burning herbs or incense, then burn it, and bury the ashes. Four elements, one disposal, it's all good.

Portal Potty

P ortals are very real, very scary metaphysical
phenomena. Chances are you have never
seen one. The civilian who asks you for help
with one has definitely never seen one.

Portals, the real kind, are opened by powerful
mages, usually by accident. Some idiot mages
think that they have opened a portal when they
have opened a gate, and vice versa. A gate is a
space through which energy is transferred. A portal is a space through which matter is transferred. I
have seen both, and I'm not being facetious when
I say that, statistically, not a one of my readers will
ever see one.

Portals are unidimensional tears in space/time.
If you see one from the side or from behind, you
see nothing. If you see one from straight on, you
see a glowing field of energy, usually blue or or-

ange, that makes audible crackling noises and emits low frequency radiation that can make you ill, and will make some materials the area the portal appears in radioactive. You can take a radiation detector and locate where a portal has been. Unfortunately for us, finding a pile of radioactive materials is not a proof of metaphysical activity, so no Randi prize there.

Portals will burn out every roll of film in a camera, and any other film near them. I have not attempted to photograph them digitally, but if I get the opportunity I will certainly try. I would assume an electromagnetic pulse is probably part of the portal's energetic exterior, so I don't have high hopes for success.

They are, without a doubt, the rarest and most dangerous of metaphysical events. They are also incredibly short lived, requiring a major expenditure of energy to come into existence. They have been torn in space by atomic blasts, the deaths of great mages and the sudden destruction of a number of lives, such as acts of terrorism.

Mages who are emergency personnel (and a lot of us are) generally leave portals alone, since most last less than a minute and will fold on their own. Those that persist for more than a minute can be destroyed very simply. All you have to do is take any empty or mostly empty vessel and pass it through the ring of energy at the portal's circumference. Since portals are unstable and require energy to persist, the empty vessel will shake the foundation of the portal enough to collapse it the vast majority of the time.

Indeed, if this does not work, I encourage you to get the heck out of there, because if you were a mage with the levels of power required to combat the type of person or thing that could make a portal durable enough to persist through such an action, you probably would not be reading this book, except perhaps for its comedic value. If you toss an empty vessel through a portal, do not stand by if said vessel does not vanish.

A word of caution, here. Portals produce enough ionizing radiation to kill you. If you go through one, you will probably die. If you do not die, you will probably get cancer or radiation poisoning and wish you were dead. They are one way passages, and they lead to dead. Powerful mages wishing to move from one plane of existence to another convert matter into pure energy and transport that energy through the friendlier phenomenon known as a gate.

If your civilian client is pointing to a spot in the empty air and claiming it is a portal, explain to them that it is absolutely not a portal. Portals are *observable*, and *everyone* in the vicinity of one will see it. If only your client can see it, it is not a portal. If you can only see it with second sight, it is not a portal. If it is not emitting noise and radiation and does not develop film, it is not a portal.

More than 90% of the time, your civilian client will be pointing at a phenomenon that exists in their head alone and saying portal. The other ten percent of the time you are looking at weather phenomena, gates and energy creatures. Weather phenomena generally aren't yours to affect and energy creatures will be dealt with later, so that leaves gates.

Gates are lesser phenomena than Portals, and are very rarely visible. If they are visible, it tends to be as a faint glow around the area of the gate, or a strange swirl if mist or smoke is present. For the most part, nothing will get by the gate without the permission of the holder of the property it appears on, so if the gate appears in a civilian's apartment, you can bet that the civilian wants it there, for whatever sick reason.

The Principle of Sympathy is the easiest mechanism to use when dealing with a gate. Using glue or tape, trace the outline of the gate with ribbon, then pull the ribbon closed, dragging the edge of the gate with it. If it is a particularly stubborn gate, sewing the ribbon with a silver needle and cotton or silk thread will usually work.

After you've moved the energetic edges of the gate, use a sealing pentagram, or a sealing hexagram, to strengthen the space where the gate had been.

It is very important that you find the source of the gate and see that it does not happen again. A civilian with a gate is sort of like a toddler with car keys. It's unlikely anything will happen, but something terrible *can* happen.

The Dispossessed

P ossession is nine-tenths of the law, and ten-elevenths a psychological phenomena explainable as schizophrenia. The rest of the time, possession is either the delusion of someone with power over the allegedly possessed person or a cry for attention. Perhaps less than 0.0000001% of the time, it involves the actual entry of an energy being into a human host. In these instances, the welcoming of the spirit into the body is voluntary, and the ability to remove the spirit also so, although the possessed usually neither believes that nor desires to eject the spirit.

This is the vital quality you must understand before attempting to deal with an allegedly possessed person… they are completely capable of expelling the energy being on their own and are unwilling to do so, either because to do so will

take away a benefit of the possession or because
they have been taught that they need an exorcism
to get better. These exorcism cravers are very
rarely satisfied by anything a normal mage can do,
so I recommend finding some Catholic Priests and
making it their problem.

Let's assume your civilian is not claiming to be
Legion and doesn't need some guy in a black suit
or a purple dress. Let's leave *De Exorcismis et Sup-
plicationibus Quibusdam* in our glove compart-
ment where it belongs and deal with the lesser
possession, people who think that they have a
lesser spirit in them making decisions for them
and making them question their judgment. If
you're clever (and you are) you will recognize this
as a classical self-esteem problem.

Of course, if you tell the civilian with low self
esteem that they have low self esteem, not a possession, you're going to make their self esteem
worse, so a small ritual with just enough magic for

them to detect it is a good compromise. I find that explaining to them that the next iteration of this ritual, should this form not work, will involve the sacrifice of a pet or human being makes them desire to have this iteration work.

There are two basic skills at removing spirits from people, and in making people who have no spirit in them but think they have a spirit in them get rid of it. You may either extract the spirit or imagined spirit into yourself and destroy it or use it to your purpose or extract it into an empty vessel or out through a gate.

The first step in both is for the possessed person to enumerate why this spirit is not welcome inside of them. A version of the *Hic, non Expectata Vos Es* (HEVE) rite works really well here. Look into the allegedly possessed person's eyes and have them state why the spirit has to go. As they state each reason, never breaking eye contact, send a small pulse of energy from their hands towards their head and repeat the charge, followed by "you are not welcome here."

For example, if your civilian states that the being has made them make bad choices, you would state "For making bad choices, leave this body, you are not welcome here." As you go through the list, steadily increase the volume, speaking at the vibrational pitch of the room. The combination of energy, volume and vibrational pitch will sway any civilian, and will push out all but the most stubborn of beings. If you use the HEVE in Latin, use a sealing octogram with the syllables of the HEVE on the person's head and heart to seal the deal.

The HEVE represents the sealing octogram and is in the order it is in to potentiate the energies of the octogram. What's nice about the HEVE is that it is a symbol of will, not of a god or being, so it is ecumenical at best. I like the HEVE because civilians think Latin is terribly, terribly metaphysical and it's really easy Latin.

If the HEVE doesn't work, and your civilian is actually dealing with an energy being, it's time to switch tactics to privation. You can literally starve or sweat an energy being out. The problem is that most people (very stupid people) believe that energy beings are less susceptible to pain and discomfort than human are. Energy beings are not used to physical discomfort. A bad cavity, stubbing your toe or a migraine headache is far more than enough to make most beings head for the hills.

You can use this to your advantage, by placing your possessed person in safe and increasing amounts of pain, while using a LBRP, HEVE or circle to make the energies of the host less and less compatible with the being inside. If you don't have a suitable vessel for them to go into, they will hold tighter, but they will still be easily dislodged without significant damage to the host.

It's important to realize that the vast majority of possessions really are mental illness, and should be handled by professionals. Don't be afraid that you'll be accused of being crazy for reporting a friend's mental illness. Most psychiatric professionals are totally willing to let harmless and content crazy people walk around unmolested, and they aren't going to care about what *you* believe.

Not-So Diviners

Tarot cards, Ouija Boards, introspection, pendula and scrying can all be very valuable tools for divining your current existence, the way things could progress in the future and the forces in play that have affected things in the past. People with too little skill in divination often end up caught in a destructive cycle in which the simplest of life decisions, like what to wear, requires the use of metaphysics to decide, and important decisions like marriage or careers are made by the swing of a pendulum.

Our not-very divine diviners are essentially addicted to removing responsibility for their actions from themselves, and a mage asked to approach a person with this problem set has to balance the person's addiction and the risk of becoming part of the same crutch. The last thing you want is to become the decision maker for a person like this.

My experience with this came from a stunning young woman who had a premonition on September 11th, 2001, and did not go to her job in Lower Manhattan. In over six years of trying, I have not heard of a single Pagan or mage killed on that day, and I find that very striking! That being said, she took this premonition to mean that her safety was largely a function of finding the desires of the spirit world and conforming to them.

By the time I came on the scene, she was already nearly agoraphobic, because she'd seen in the Tarot cards that see was going to die if she went outside. Since the cards didn't give her a timeline, any time she went outside and lived, she considered herself to have dodged a bullet and that it was the next time that she would die.

Trying to tell her we all die sometime did not get me very far, so we ended up having to do multiple tarot readings, with carefully worded queries that would make her either more likely to come out or have no effect at all. Eventually, over a period of weeks, I convinced her that interpretation of the reading that she felt indicated death was actually discussing change, a common misconception by readers. She eventually conformed to my vision and stopped being afraid to leave, but she still had this idea that everything that had to be decided required the aid of a scrying or divining device.

The New Age Market culture creates this phenomenon, because it profits by it. It took a very long time, but eventually I convinced her that she was under the spell of a powerful wizard, and that spell had convinced her that she could not make up her mind for herself. I performed the sealing octogram on her, as well as the HEVE, and eventually she became convinced that she had pushed the bad spell away.

After a few months without her pendula and cards, she'd began to see what a fool she had been, but she was one of the lucky ones. Many civilians who get stuck in this mental trap never get out, and this can be especially bad if the person has a prediction about the future that is especially dire and can only end in the death of one person or another.

The problem with this is that your average civilian *has* a little bit of magical talent, so when they are sitting here building up this power it sometimes sticks and makes their obsession reality. This is why you have to utterly convince them of the error of their belief, because that stupid little fragment of power they have is all that it will take to potentiate their ridiculous premonition.

To replace a premonition in someone's mind, you need to use the power of persuasion to talk them out of it, and you need to use the Principle of Sympathy to change their premonition. This requires some skill, because you need to create the premonition not the incident itself. By creating a simulacrum of wax and hair you can focus your will on implanting a new premonition. I find the old fashioned technique of making the simulacrum our of beeswax with a knot of hair at the heart (or a drop of blood) and talking to it as if it were the person to actually be more effective than some of the "voodoo doll" ceremonies you'll find online.

Once you have it made, simply tell it, on a regular basis, that it is not going to die on the seventeenth of March or whatever the premonition wrecking your civilian's life is. The causal link of the hair and the principal of Sympathy, plus your own innate power, really is enough to fully empower it.

Rather than think of it as doing an old fashioned, simplistic rite, I like to think of wax simulacra as kicking it old school. They are not the most effective thing for massive energy work, but they are very functional as foci for smaller uses of energy. Implanting a compulsion or idea in a civilian's head is just about the smallest use of energy there is. They have set themselves up to be influenced. You are merely doing their will.

Faeries and Boggles

There are very real creatures in the world that biologists have not discovered. Many of them, such as the Jersey Devil, Bigfoot and the Yeti, are normal biological species that mages have detected while searching for portals or gates in allegedly haunted areas. It is likely that with the advent of thermal imagining we will soon see these mysteries solved conclusively. These matter organisms differ from energy beings in that they are detectable but hard to detect, and most of them are from our same evolutionary ladder.

A lot of people know diddly about evolution, which is a shame. Mages tend to *get it* because the powers of natural observation you need to cultivate to be mage show you that it is all around you. What a lot of people don't understand is that while all multicellular terrestrial life may share a common ancestor, no scientists believe that all the life that may exist in the whole of the universe is descended, magically, from the same critters that we came from here on *terra firma*.

Most mages believe that the fae races, the Sidhe, dragons, gods, angels and the rest are a part of a non-terrestrial phylogenic tree, or trees, or that they are an example of parallel evolution. The gods, and other beings with superior technology to mankind assuredly evolved elsewhere in the universe, although few agree as to whether they are from other planets, other planes or other dimensions. What we do agree upon is that they are not genetically related to us in the same way as dogs and cats are.

Without going into too much detail regarding the nature of our relationship to these entities, I want to explain some of our chief interactions. Faeries and boggles are terms used to describe any matter creatures that are outside of our genetic lineage but not deities. In general, the terms faeries or fae are used to describe creatures that are beneficent or neutral and the term boggle is used to describe creatures that are malicious or neutral but scary. When your civilian claims he is beset by evil faeries that are making his life impossible, it is boggles that are likely to blame.

Faeries rarely give a right damn about human beings, unless they have an exceptional talent, and the possession of exceptional talents tends to make people *not* civilians. Boggles, on the other hand, are attracted to silly people like most civilians, and feed on them and their wasteful use of energy. If someone reports an infestation of boggles around themselves, you can pretty much guarantee they've been dabbling in some new age hocus pocus and they've managed to appear just sparkly enough to let these little energy sponges start chewing on them. This generally means your civilian is going out of their mind with worry, seeing things out of the corners of their eyes, in dark closets and around turns. If you have the unfortunate situation of living with this person, their screams and freak outs will be especially grating on you, so getting it dealt with as soon as possible is a good idea.

Your first step is to make the place less boggle friendly. That means less places to hide, more light and less sparkle and sugar. Clean house, put crystals and candles away and stop leaving out food. Don't worry about pet food, because most pets are not boggle friendly and are pretty fierce about defending their food dish.

Once you've taken care of their physical comfort, you need to take care of their metaphysical comfort. That means draining the energy sources they are consuming and placing any other energy source inside a silk cloth, or silk lined box, which is where they should've been to begin with. Use sealing octograms and pentagrams to clean the space, then drive the boggles out with labdanum, asafetida or sagebrush. Once they are gone, use a paintbrush to paint a line of iron infused water (see materiel) all the way around the room. Make a double line at the doorway, and use a sealing octogram or pentagram to seal it.

Draw a similar line around the sash of every window and around every door. If necessary, repeat the procedure for the entire house. You can also do this when painting or cleaning a new residence. Seal the windows and doors.

For a conjury or a ritual space, I find a combination of iron infused water, blood and holy water is more than sufficient. I do not recommend using your blood on spaces that are not yours, as it tells various nasty critters that this space is protected by *your* body and will. If you have a particularly stupid civilian under your protection you're just welcoming trouble by placing them under your blood's seal.

If your civilian's hysteria is seeing boggles from inside a car, or outside their windows, a simple spray bottle of the iron infused water and a really simple attention turning spell will work wonders. I find wording the spell in such a way that you essentially state "do not see what you are not meant to see" is enough.

Spray the car windows, or other glass, with a fine mist of iron infused water. Make sure to tell the civilian that the water will stop them from seeing the boggles, since it's likely more than half of what they see does not exist outside their mind.

Indigo Blues

A reoccurring problem for mages of all sorts is whenever the popular press gets hold of an old idea and mangles it. We've seen this in the past ten years with Wicca, the past thirty or so with magic and the past five with the idea of the "indigo children."

The creators of the indigo concept were a mild and wacky synesthete and a channeler who spoke to an alleged mystic entity named Kryon. They came up with the idea that ill-behaved children don't have ADHD, or special needs, instead they have mystic powers. A good friend of mine and synesthete in her own right is sort of an authority on these things because as a child she was an intensely studied "gifted and talented" kid, and today she's a mage and scientist. She meets *every* qualification that the indigo authors have listed for an indigo, and as a synesthete can even see the so-called "auras" that the indigo authors claim the mystic beams leave behind.

She's also most definitely the highest functioning autistic person in the world, and her weirdness as a child, sensitivity to light and sound, attitude and sense of entitlement were fully a function of having an IQ two standard deviations above the mean and an autistic spectrum disorder. If anyone would be relieved to find out they had mystic beams that set them apart, this person would be, and she contends that it is absolutely impossible that she is an "Indigo." She says this because she's a scientist, and a mage, and if anyone could detect special kids, scientists and mages could.

Now, I'm no scientist, but I am a mage, and I can tell you that not only are Indigos fake, but the entire Indigo movement is full of lies. Pick up books on the movement and you will see people say it's caused by cosmic radiation, but proven scientifically (it hasn't been) or that it's not the result of channeling or anything psychic (although it is, according to others) or that it's the new age, or whatever. It can't be all these things at once!

What Indigo really is, however, is an elaborate and very real deception to make the incredibly smart feel better about themselves. These super geniuses need to feel better about themselves, because they understand a lot more than the rest of humankind, and one of the first things they learn is that being smart is not something that the bulk of the population considers good. It's also a way of helping adults who are not capable of fully understanding their genius kids. Scientists who've studied genius kids and adults realize very early on that a few things hinder the super smart in their attempts to fit in. Chief amongst these problems are:

1. They see sexuality as causing a lot of difficulty for "normals" and either avoid it or

approach it in ways that are beyond the norm. Jealousy tends to not be a problem, monogamy and sexual orientation are not strictly defined or of major importance.

2. They tend to be comfortable with ambiguity, and often see more than one side of an issue, making them feel as if they are the only ones who understand an issue.

3. The higher understanding allows for a strong understanding of fairness, and often an expectation that people will behave in fair ways. This leads to disappointment and sometimes bitterness.

4. Super genius kids tend to be self-motivated. This means that things contrary to their motivation, including homework and chores, will often be neglected. A child can have an IQ significantly above the mean and fail every class they take.

5. Since they have a specialist, not generalist, approach to learning, they will often be B students without ever getting a B...they either do well in a class or fail it, or do the minimum needed to pass a class. They may even find they get low grades in classes that hold their interest if the grades are based on the foundational concepts behind the details that interest them. In college, they may nearly fail every class at the freshman level, and ace every class at the senior or higher level.

6. They tend to understand a theory before they understand how it works, so they learn "backwards" compared to other kids.

7. They enjoy making personal rules or building schedules and plans. They often don't follow them, being more interested in figuring out the most effective ways to do a thing than doing the thing.

8. They are capable of reducing incredibly complex processes into simple step-wise plans, lists or procedures, and often have little patience for those who cannot follow their procedures.

9. They have a wide variety of interests, and will often seem to randomly do well in classes—acing math one year and failing it the next as their interests wax and wane.

10. They have a mistrust of things they have no understanding of, which is an increasingly small list of things as they age.

11. Their parents often feel like they are creatures from another planet, and the kids believe it!

12. They may do exceedingly well, or exceedingly poorly, on IQ tests, as IQ tests get less accurate the further from the mean you are. An "outside the box" kid may

score 180 and 80 on the same test on different dates.

If your civilian has become convinced that he, or his genius children, are Indigos, be prepared for an uphill battle. Parents of Indigos are worried about stepping on their kid's fragile egos, so they refuse to properly discipline them. I once watched an Indigo at a park physically beat the crap out of another kid while the mother told the child that he should stop and he was violating the kid's personal space. An appropriate mother would've scruffed the kid like a naughty kitten and pulled him off.

If an otherwise sane mother can come up with the idea that pulling their hellion off of an innocent victim somehow hurts said hellion, you can imagine what other complete nonsense they might come up with. Remember, always, that Mother of Indigo spells out MOI, moi, French for ME. The mother of an Indigo says it is about her child, but it is about her, about how special and wonderful and talented she is. (MOI can just as easily, but less often, be a Dad.)

While the MOI is likely to not believe anything that discounts her wackiness, the easiest way to tell that a child does not operate at a high energy level is to place a so-called television stone (a type of Ulexite) on the child's forehead. If an untrained person operates at a high energy level, the Ulexite will glow slightly, and this can be detected by even the least en-ergetic of people. People who use their energy, even poorly, tend to not emit unless they are doing it on purpose.

In fact, getting a piece of Ulexite to glow is a good trick for mages to learn. It's a trial and error sort of thing, but with enough practice you'll be able to do it with ease. Simply hold the Ulexite in your hand and push energy to your hand. The Ulexite will sort of sparkle, reflecting the skin and the energy around it.

But what if the MOI isn't claiming their obnoxious brat is an Indigo? What if they are claiming that their child is the reincarnation of a Lama or King Arthur or Jesus or something like that? That can be pretty scary. Just as in the possession problem, these parents have given up on their own dreams and are now using their children as a vessel for all their hopes and dreams. They are the stage parents of metaphysics, and no matter how clearly you state that Johnny is a normal grub, not the second coming, they aren't going to believe you.

Some claims are easier to refute than others. The Second Coming of Jesus would have Jesus powers. The Reincarnation of King Arthur can summon the Lady of the Lake in any pure water and can touch the Crying Stone and have it call out the end to the current monarchy. Also, when he gets a cold, Britain suffers, The Secret of the Grail, remember, is that The King and The Land are one.

Changelings are the easiest to identify of all. Salt and iron will burn them, and if you boil water in an eggshell they are supposed to reveal themselves by custom and incredulity. Since the MOI is invested in their kid being special because *they* gave birth to something special, most of them won't claim their kid is a changeling.

Since Indigos are (intentionally!) classified as being difficult to classify, the fact that they fail the descriptions of Indigos given in books and on websites is no problem for the MOI. If she's very invested in the whole living-the-life-through-the-child paradigm, you're not going to be able to help. Since she thinks her kid is super-special, she will fall victim to the same Little Emperor problem we've seen in China. If she has more than one child, and only feels that one of them is a special individual, her preferential treatment of the one may border on outright child abuse for the other. People of good conscience should report child abuse to the authorities when they see it.

The good news is that most of these MOIs are deceived, and nasty, but they aren't true Svengalis, and they've decided to seek their attention this way, instead of developing things like Munchausen-by-Proxy. At worst, the kid will grow up into a brat that society will eventually discipline. At best, the kid will grow up to read this book.

Levitation Levity

Any one who watched Saturday morning cartoons when a child knows that the secret to levitation is not understanding gravity, or wearing a turban and chanting sim sim salla bim! Our civilians, however, think levitation is the ultimate in proof of one's magic ability, therefore they believe it in others and expect it in you.

Yes, you and I and David Blaine use variations on Balducci to levitate ourselves when we need a quick gimmick. This is the same technique used by Sherpa and Yogis, because to maintain it requires some small bit of skill and some clever thinking ahead. If you want a civilian to believe you when you are dealing with something terribly uncomfortable, like the fact that they are not possessed or their kid isn't an Indigo, a good way to get their trust is to levitate for them, and Balducci is a trick you can learn on the internet.

I knew a Yogi who could do for-real levitation. He sat on a towel wherever you asked him to, and once levitated, you could pull the towel out from underneath him. His technique required a ridiculous amount of energy, and he achieved this energy by sucking the energy from the people around him. The more skeptical the people were, the less energy he got. He made a fairly good living at this, about $30,000 American dollars a year, and put five street kids through college. I tried to convince him to try for the Randi Prize, but he was of a religious sect that eschewed monetary gain. Most of his raised money went to charities.

If he was using an illusion, he was using magic to make us think he was not using an illusion, and that's a heck of a thing. Levitation is a disgustingly large expenditure of energy, and if you do use magic to levitate, you're going to find you lack the energy to do much else. I suppose it's alright as a sort of magical masturbation, but I think that if you're using it to do anything other than gain a million dollars from a skeptic you're wasting your time.

Mystic levitation involves causing one of three effects– the rushing of air, providing lift; the creation of magnetic poles, creating the ability to repulse; and the creation of ultrasonic noise, creating acoustic levitation. Each of these may be practiced individually at the small scale using small non-magnetic objects, like rubber balls. I've seen people successfully pull off all three mechanisms with extensive practice.

When a civilian comes to you concerned about their own levitation, they are generally referring to the parlor game known as "light as a feather, stiff as a board." This is a combination of hypnosis and simple distribution of weight used by teenage girls. While some variations upon it tell the levitated person to imagine their death (which can result in the same problem we saw with civilians and predestination, earlier) most forms merely involve chanting and lifting with one's fingers.

The average young teenage girl is under 80 pounds. Without the chanting, a group of five girls need only shoulder twenty pounds a piece to lift their friend. Since they have chanted to get their actions in unison, the lifting is accomplished by all girls, including the "stiff as a board" one at the same time. As the girls lift, the liftee literally bends like a concave lens (the human body does this easily) allowing the girls to lift approximately 25% (or five pounds each) of the weight of the liftee's body. When the liftee realizes, consciously or not, that she is bending, and straightens out, the girls feel an increase in weight, usually up to about 20lbs. They take this as having "broken concentration," and the liftee falls with an audible thunk.

Since children are little power sinks, there is always the possibility that 2-3 of the lifters are, in fact, using magic to help themselves lift, possibly reducing the weight of the liftee again by half. The results are rarely any different, but the children will feel very tired and irritable afterwards. This is partially responsible for the urban mythology of "Light as a Feather, Stiff as a board" that includes all sorts of terrible things happening afterwards, like possessions and random lights flickering and poltergeist activity. These are actually the kids trying to re-equilibrate their power after a sudden use of it.

Poltergeist activity is nearly always the result of strong and untrained mages, especially wild talents or therions, and many of these are young, female and terribly hormonal. In my experience, young females who do not generate any poltergeist activity are actually less common than those that do. Most of these poltergeist activities are slight, the occasional door that slams without reason, glasses that break in cabinets, streetlights and lightbulbs that go out or even burst unexpectedly. The only cure for this is for the girl (or, less often, boy) to control their emotions or energies via magical training or meditation.

If the civilian having the trouble with poltergeists is a parent, you run the risk of causing harm to the child if you point out the activity is caused by the child. You must use caution as you train the child while protecting them from their civilian parent. Often, suggesting that meditation or yoga will help the parent better when the whole family participates is a good way to rein a child's nascent powers in. As the teacher of teachers says, "Caution must be your Watchword."

Energy Beings

Most life forms on Earth are primarily matter beings, but the higher order matter beings generally possess a large electrical generating unit, such as the mammalian brain. Energy beings are beings that bypass the matter stage of existence and go right into the energy stage, existing as energy and information. Some fringe scientists are starting to get a real clue about the existence of life. It is not water or heat that causes life to exist, it is energy. Soon, science may be indistinguishable from magic.

It is possible for self-replicating compounds to come into existence wherever they have the building blocks of their compounds and energy. This energy can be heat or magnetism, radioactive decay, gravity, light or any number of things that cause there to be an energetic state. If you bounce enough molecules around in such a system, the energy of these compounds will cause some of them to stick together. Reach a high enough level of complexity, and you get life.

Energy beings are self-replicating energetic forces. They generally require a medium to exist within, and they can be found wherever a large quantity of energy is generated. They vary in sentience from barely sentient self-replicating compounds that attach themselves to areas of large static or electrical energy and only show up in our environment accidentally to penultimately potent beings that probably evolved from matter systems similar to ours but now exist as energy constructs.

Philosophically, animals on this planet are transitional species. We have a matter substrate, our bodies, but the real "stuff" of our being exists in the complex electrical structures of the nervous system. Non-electrical life, such as plants, don't have complex electrical currents, and thus are understood as being non-energy beings. How you differ from a tree is how a purely energetic being differs from you. A mouse, however, differs nearly as much as you do from a tree, so you can imagine the scope of these beings.

Most energy beings, the insects of the energy world, are simple self-replicating collections of forces. We perceive them as lights, zones of ionized air, background errors in radiation detection, unexplained blobs of heat on infrared cameras and strange sensations. Since humans are very limited in the ability to detect energy, especially compared to other animals on this planet, we don't tend to perceive these energy beings unless we are doing something that includes energy detection. Soldiers using thermoimaging goggles, for example, regularly see "sneeches" and boggles that go away merely by rubbing their eyes or resetting the goggles, but these boggles don't appear in highly shielded environments, ruling out the idea that they are purely random.

It's very funny that our civilians, even when soldiers in other realms, can be so very convinced that they are in error that they will ignore something that is detectable, replicable and often a shared experience, seeing it as an error rather than something they don't have words for. It's funny, and a little scary.

If energy beings are infesting an area and causing trouble, they can be dealt with by creating your own fields of energy or disrupting theirs. Primarily electrical beings can be disrupted by electricity and strong magnetism, drained off with grounding wires, bounced or dispersed with conducting materials or blockaded with strong insulators. Beings of light can be forced away by creating a sheet of light in an opposite direction to theirs.

Both of these things require very simplistic set up and can be accomplished with mirrors and light sources or with wires and batteries. Connecting a wire to one end of a small battery and another wire to the other is the simplest barricade against electrical energy beings, and using simple EMP shielding techniques, such as Faraday Boxes, will keep sensitive equipment secure from them. If you make your own Faraday Boxes out of mylar or aluminum and cardboard, people may think you're one of those tinfoil hat people. A really elegant work around that will not seem quite so paranoid is a cast iron box, with the item inside protected against energy by a thick layer of insulating silk. One mage of repute I am aware of keeps a highly energetic item in an antique cast iron box inscribed with protective sigils. The item inside is wrapped tightly in thick silk, and then rests buried within 3 inches of rock salt. This item is thus protected from most boggles, changelings, EMPs and casual contact. I don't think the object warrants that level of protection, but it certainly has it.

Remember, *most* energy beings are not particularly aware of your existence and don't care to bother you. If you see them, it's generally not intentional. They aren't there to warn you or scare you or anything like that, they just are there.

High level energy beings, like most gods and most things considered angels are beyond the scope of this book and should be dealt with according to theology and the expertise of others. Remember, if you are not 100% sure of what you're doing, you're a civilian. Mages do things for reasons. Even if you're experimenting, use controls and take notes. Don't be a dabbler.

If your civilian has started encountering energy beings and making a fuss, you need to draw the beings off and convince the civilian they are wrong. Being shown the existence of such things is very damaging to civilians, because their little worlds are houses built on sand. Convince a civilian that energy beings are real and they freak out even worse than most people do at the sight of a mouse.

If you're ever dealt with mice, you know the best way of dealing with them is to get rid of their food supply, seal off their access routes and get a cat or terrier (or, I suppose, a large snake.) You can also choose to live with them, as they are more a nuisance than anything else.

Energy beings can be a nuisance and are easier to get rid of than mice. You need to cut off their food supply (disrupting large sources of energy with shielding or by removing the energy altogether, removing ionized air with de-ionizing filters or humidifiers.) Eliminate their access (paint rooms with paint with a high percentage of metal, such as magnetic primer or any high-quality primer with a high level of titanium; use window screens of stainless steel or copper mesh instead of plastic in windows are to be open regularly) and get things that feed on them.

Small, non-sentient energy beings are disrupted by water, which is why many mages have aquaria of various sizes and shapes. Salt water is particularly effective at grounding a room, but can make a room too humid. Don't be afraid to install a humidity monitor in a room with an aquarium, and don't be afraid to take up fish collecting for its fringe benefits.

Astralism and Angels

Angels are energy beings of the highest order, and tend to be beyond the ken of most mages. Like people, they have religions, and while some use the term angels to refer to Abrahamic angels, Hellenic daimons and other high-energy beings, I prefer the term daimons, because the term refers to any non-god energy of a place, including sentient ones. "Genii" is also a good term, in the Latin sense, but the term is confused with the Arabic djinn enough to render the term useless for our purposes.

Many civilians in the New Age movements confuse Astralism (or Astral Travel) with guided meditation or spirit quests, and the differences between the two from the standpoint of the civilian's experience are negligible, but the dangers and the civilian's potential for self-harm are *not* the same. In Astralism, the human converts his essence into a temporary energy being and is capable of perceiving energy beings in their natural state. As an energy being, the human is susceptible to the forms of disruption we use against energy beings. A person in an Astral state is capable of being severely energetically damaged by electrical and magnetic fields, energy beings who are in their natural states and more competent mages.

While the urban myth of cutting the silver cord and killing the body is just that, significant damage while in an Astral form can lead to problems with the body's electrical system, causing neurological symptoms and conditional such as M.S., Parkinson's Disease, brain and spinal cancers and forms of heart disease that involve the electric circuitry of the heart. Psychiatric disorders such as schizophrenia and bipolar disorder are also common effects of damage while in an astral form, and the damage is very much cumulative. Mages with early stages of these conditions, or a genetic tendency towards them should avoid Astralism, as should those in a strained relationship with greater energy beings, including gods. Many a mage in hot water with his ancestors or gods has been damaged in an astral form by an entity with nothing but good intentions.

While Astralism is possible, the vast majority of what a civilian does is guided meditation or spirit walking, in which he imagines himself assuming an animal or energy form and traveling on a journey. Those who have done both have no difficulty distinguishing between the two: one goes inward, to a place of very minor danger and helpful guides and angels who often save the meditating person just when the end is nigh; the other goes outward, to a place of little danger and mostly neutral creatures and in which if things should actually go pear-shaped, genuine damage is completely possible.

The external observer can tell the states apart easily, if he has enough technology or the ability to visualize energy. The Astral form will be capable of being seen on infrared, if only fleetingly, and will disturb electrical fields. Things like fluorescent lights, which are very sensitive to such things, are simple to affect when in an Astral form. If you hook an Astral person to a biological monitor, you will find that they show electrical impulses similar to the comatose or deeply drugged.

Those traveling within, instead of without, do not create energy fields normally, and they also do not give the signs of being drugged or comatose. If you hook them to a bioelectrical monitor, they will show waves similar to those they show when telling a story or when dreaming. The trip in this instance, like those accomplished with hallucinogens, is into an internal space.

This internal space is actually more instructive than the external space of Astalism, and the beings met within, including angels and daimons, and even the spirits of the dearly departed come from within the mind of the traveler, not from without.

To become accustomed to this inner world, good metaphysical teachers always begin with guided meditation, usually involving intensive visualization using multiple senses and headspaces. Exploring these boundaries teaches the mage to develop a very strong, forceful inner world in which he or she can construct a reality that the mage can then impose, by sheer force of will, upon the rest of the universe. Without the visualization skill, no one can become even a half-way decent mage, regardless of their innate power level.

If your civilian is claiming to have met a god or angel, you need to seriously consider the distinct probability that your civilian in fact *visualized* that deity or angel, and that the edicts the angel, god, totem or so-called "spirit guide" gave the civilian are nothing more or less than the civilian's attempt to rationalize a change in his or her behavior.

If the change is positive, there is no reason for you, as the mage, to dissuade the civilian from believing he spoke to a guardian angel or other powerful external spirit, as he is tapping a place of inner strength and is eventually going to figure out his being came from within. Even if he never gets it, he's only helped himself by doing these things, so it works out fine in the end. Your job, as a professional mage in a world of civilians, is to make your dabbler as harmless as possible, and to point him as far from real power as possible. Let him think his guilty conscience is the archangel Gabriel, as long as it castrates him and keeps him away from professionals. Let him play with nonsense things like Ouija Boards, he can't hurt himself or people who matter.

If this sounds cynical, it perhaps is a bit. There are real energy beings, real angels and gods, real "demons" and daimons, real Genii and Djinn, but they are not going to involve themselves with a civilian for the same reasons that few mages will get seriously involved with a civilian... the civilian literally exists outside their world and is useless to them. The civilian does not bother the creatures that exist merely in energetic ways, they bother physical beings, things like you and I.

There is no greater discretion you will have to learn than when to agree with the civilian's bogus interpretation of events and when to let them go. You will have to cultivate this ability carefully, because if they see cynicism they will cease to believe you.

So what if Johnny One-Spell claims his guardian angel comes to him when he uses special Guardian Angel summoning oil and swears to remain chaste until he's married. Johnny's not hurting anyone. At the worst, his goofiness keeps him from breeding another civilian, and that can only be a good thing.

It is acceptable to squash hard upon a civilian or mage who abuses the gullibility of others for a profit, especially if you find it morally repugnant. Be aware, however, that pointing out this stuff publicly will make civilians dangerously aware that there are real supernatural critters. If you, for example, ask for replicable results on a specially-marketed angel ritual, but are publicly a mage, you are telling a smart civilian that magic is replicable, and can be studied in scientific terms.

Admittedly, civilians are generally stupid enough to think that means magic is associated with whatever PBS special is hot right now, so you'll hear this means magic is explained by Quantum Physics, String Theory or Quorum Seeking. The statistical chances of a civilian figuring *anything* out without a huge number of mages screwing up in identical ways are slim to none,

and probably not worth worrying about.

Afterword

This book contains exactly three lies, and in the interest of protecting civilians who somehow pick this book up, I will not tell you which statements are lies and which are truths. I intend to invoke the Paradox of Truthful Lies. There are lies here, and truths, and I will not tell a soul which are which, merely that they number three. This could, itself, be a lie, but it isn't....unless it is.[1]

This book is actually quite dangerous in the wrong hands, in the hands of a civilian who *wants* to believe in magic, and has a sub-mage level of natural energy. It contains a subtext of tips which can be used to root out mages who are private about their magic, or who outright claim to do no magic, despite doing magic regularly. I believe this

---

[1] It isn't.

subtext is significantly hidden and beyond the ken of most civilians, who are generally stupid.

By finding this book, you're either a mage or a civilian who is inordinately lucky. Since no civilian will understand this book, and since no one completely failing to understand this book will read this far, I think we're generally safe. In short, this book should've taught you the following lesson, which only a mage will fully grasp: *Magic is real, possible, powerful, detectable, discernable, replicable and provable. It exists with rules, techniques and laws, and at the same time does not do the things that the skeptical people will accept as magic.*

It took nearly one-thousand years for the knowledge of the true nature of the philosopher's stone to become public knowledge, despite Hermes Trismegistus telling people of the transformations it created in no uncertain terms. If this unhidden secret, or Truthful Lie, can be lost on the general public despite coming up on any search engine on the first few pages, I don't think an independent book, from a tiny press, from an unknown author, is going to do anyone any damage.

Nonetheless, I know that I will have gravely offended some mages with this book, either because they believe in some of the nonsense geared towards civilians and found herein or because they think I have revealed truths that may be oathbound to their particular field of magic. Nothing in here is discussed that is oathbound in any tradition or fraternal organization *to which I belong.* They may be held as secret to other groups, but since I am not a member, and have no way of proving they exist in those groups I am therefore not culpable.

I will say to those with ears to hear that there are likely to be those who will do everything possible to see that this book does not end up in anyone's hands. I am fully prepared for vicious attacks upon myself and the contents of this book, and for this reason I ask that you mention this book only to those who you *know* are safe. The enemies, idiot civilians who have taken offense, mages who think I've revealed too much and mages who think I haven't revealed enough, will attack this book if they find out about it.

If you know, and you will, and you dare, then by the love of all that is, keep silent!

Techniques

The techniques herein are a handful of rites I have mentioned in passing and which I feel capable of giving to the beginning mage who has managed somehow to find this work. Not all of the techniques are described herein, and, in fact, I have deliberately laid clues only to some techniques, rather than engage in the oath-breaking of others.

LBRP: Lesser Banishing Ritual of The Pentagram

The LBRP is the worst hidden non-public ritual in all of magic. You can search on the acronym LBRP or the term itself and probably come up with a correct version of the rite within a few pages. If you come upon a version that is Pagan-friendly, or non-Abrahamic in nature, you've found a fraud....the rest I leave to you.

To properly learn the LBRP, you need to be shown the energetic states associated with the acronym involved. There are versions on the web that will tell you to "attune" one of the syllables or "vibrate" them, and these are useful if and only if you've experienced someone else doing it. If you exist in a tense relationship with the entity in question, or do not believe in it, or are a Diabolist, or perhaps a non-Jewish Abrahamicist, you are playing with energies that you've no business dabbling with. Ex-Abrahamic mages are best off doing something that does not resonate with their life.

Nonetheless, the energetic symbology involved can be easily enough replicated in various other forms without invoking any god, or by invoking many. The Pentalpha of the Olympiad is a powerful and similar rite that invokes Apollo, Athena, Poseidon, Zeus and Hades as well as the inner strengths of mind over matter, mind over strength, strength over matter, mind over strength and matter over all. This ritual must be trained in to be understood, but I have provided enough information for a lone practitioner to reconstruct a working version if his gods and the gods of the Greeks are the same.

Three By Three Purification

The Three By Three purification in this book on page 26 is useful for things other than the Ouija Board. Using the details on that and following pages, any mage worth his salt (and water) should be able to work out a version for other items.

HEVE: "hic, Non expectata vos es"

The HEVE is a little better hidden than the LBRP, and can be used in a similar way. If may take some experience to work this out from the description, but it's really very elegant.

To do a HEVE without a sealing octogram, focus your energies in the now, and with your hands held at face level, palms out as if you are saying "stop," intone "Hic!" (here) It should come out as a single powerful syllable, and as you say it, throw your hands down, casting energy towards the earth. Force the entities being banished to confront the fact that they, as non-natural residents of the physical plane are weaker than you, as a natural resident.

Cross your arms as you declare "Non expectata" (Are not welcomed, are not expected, are not permitted), and feel the energy inside yourself and in the world that makes the wrongness right. Gather the reflection of the way the world should be into your consciousness, and hold it in your active hand. If you are ambidexterous, hold it in your writing hand or the one you eat with most often.

Use your left or passive hand to point at the entity in question, and intone "vos" (you) in a way that you direct the attention of the universe upon the entity in question. A talented mage can sometimes imply the whole of the HEVE with a "you" and a pointed finger.

Once you have drawn the attention of the universe to the entity, take the reality that should be and inflict it upon the entity with a strong "es," making the form of the verb "to be" a command and the end of the spell. If you really know your will, you can usually accomplish enough with the HEVE to not need to do it more than once.

Sealing Pentagrams, Octograms and Hexagrams

The sealing pentagram is merely a pentagram (the direction and the direction you draw it in will vary by the purpose) used to ward or close a gap. Protecting yourself with a pentagram and drawing it on something actually requires reverse drawing directions, and the number of points up depends on whether it is a triumph of spirit over will or of will over spirit.

The pentagram is drawn with one continuous motion, with an energetic focus at each point and as the shape is closed. The Hexagram, which is familiar as the Magen David, is drawn with one hand doing a triangle, and the other doing a second, inverted in relation to the second. This can be very potent with Abrahamic entities, because of its modern usage. Paired with the LBRP you'll pretty much ward off anything under Abrahamic domain.

The sealing octogram can be drawn similarly, using the right hand for the "right" square and the left hand for the twisted square. It can be potent in warding off more recent Abrahamic entities, because of its power in Persian architecture. You can also use each of the syllables of the HEVE to sign the octogram. The four winds or elements are also capable of being added, and by making the twisted square at one-third, you can add the third triangle of the twelve-pointed star of the Olympic deities.

Both the hexagram and the octogram use the two energies of the opposing hands to dictate the

power over a space. This makes them more difficult to master than a sealing pentagram but not
necessarily more potent. Remember that each suc-
cessful sealing shape strengthens the others you
have made and each failure weakens the others
you have made. Use one for general purpose and
one for special occasions.

Materiel

The most important devices in your tool box are your will, your blood, a black knife to draw it with, silk or another insulator, salt or another purifier, incense or sagebrush to cleanse with and holy waters.

Most of these you already possess or can achieve with little work, holy waters, on the other hand, can be a terrible thing to try to get, especially if you don't live near a cathedral where dipping a flask in a font would go unnoticed. A Pagan, especially a Wiccan or a Druid, can usually whip up Solar, Lunar and Solar-Lunar holy water in a pinch, although the ideal time to whip up Solar Water is on the Summer Solstice, at the dawn before the moment of Solstice. Lunar Water is made on the night of the new moon and takes a little longer.

Solar Holy Water

Have a Druid or a Pagan with a relationship with a solar deity, a deity of inspiration, a fire deity or a "shining" deity perform this rite. They should invoke the name of their deity as appropriate during the creation of the holy water. Ra is the classical deity for this, but should only be invoked by people with a prior relationship with him.

The water should be clean, but not distilled or filtered. Ideally, it should have a maximum potential energy as drawn, so it should come from above the most powerful waterfall you have access to, or, if that is not possible, from the cleanest spring or purest well you have access to. I recommend doing less than one gallon at a time.

The water should be transferred into a steel or iron pot and boiled for 10 minutes. It must be allowed to cool, then should be poured through a double thickness of course woven silk, or wool, or, failing that, all-cotton cheesecloth. Traditionally, each element of holy water should be dear to the maker, so use the most expensive, highest quality ingredients you can find.

The water should then be added to a broad bowl. Ideally, this is made of brass or gold. It is also possible to use a clear vase or amphora. It is covered with a black cloth, and removed to the outside font area. This place should have southern clearance, and an access to the rising sun. At the moment the sun becomes visible, remove the black cloth and hold the bowl aloft. Infuse the bowl with the morning sunlight, and invoke the blessings of the deity into the water. Bring it down, and add to the bowl a singular coin (or coin shaped piece) of the purest gold possible, one handful of salt from beneath the ground, a sprin-kling of the ashes of a laurel crown, and several drops of pure attar of roses. You may need to tweak these ingredients dependant upon your de-ity of choice.

The water must get no less than one full day of sunlight. After it has done so, but before the sun has fully set, pour the water into a gold or optically opaque flask and stopper. Cover in a piece of silk when not in use, and use within one solar year.

Using the Principle of Sympathy, you can expand this water by mixing more holy water than pure into a gold or glass vessel. This should be done during the day in full sunlight and appropriate energy should be added.

Lunar Holy Water

Have a Druid or a Pagan with a relationship with a lunar deity, a deity of truth, a water deity or a "hidden" deity perform this rite. They should invoke the name of their deity as appropriate during the creation of the holy water. Hades is the classical deity for this, but should only be invoked by people with a prior relationship with him.

Just as with the prior materiel, the water should be clean, but not distilled or filtered. Unlike the prior, however, water should be drawn from the deepest well you can find, or can be drawn from water with the highest possible expended energy, such as water from beneath a waterfall or at the end of a slow river.

Boil and filter the water as described in the prior recipe, and placed into a similar bowl, save that this bowl should be made of stone or silver. It is covered, and brought to an outdoor font area. At the moment the new moon is highest in the sky, the priest should invoke the hidden moon into the water. When that happens, he must add a silver obol (a replica is fine) to the water. The water sits under the new moon for one hour. This is repeated once a night for one month, with the following additions:

Waxing Quarter: Thirteen drops of essential oil of Night blooming Jasmine.

Half: Thirteen grains of coarse sea salt.

Full: The seed of a moonflower, or better, the fresh bloom from a moonflower.

Half: Thirteen grains of coarse sea salt.

Waning quarter: Thirteen drops of Tuberose Absolute. If you absolutely cannot get this, use more jasmine.

On the set of the next new moon, add the water to a black opaque glass flask, or barring that, a silver one. Do not expose to sunlight. It may be expanded as with Solar water, but when the moon is full. Use within one lunar year.

Solar-Lunar Holy Water

When it is dim, and the sun and the full moon both are in the sky, as during an eclipse or at sunrise, Solar and Lunar waters may be combined in a one-to-one ratio simultaneously by a priest with a relationship with both deities or by two priests. This must be done swiftly, and within an earthenware bowl.

It must be decanted into an earthenware flask, but will last for over three years if kept out of sunlight or moonlight. The most potent of the waters, it requires a person or persons whose energies are opposite but compatible.

Hellenic Holy Water

Hellenic Holy Waters flow from sacred springs or the roots of sacred trees and are gathered and consecrated by dedicants of said gods. In general, there is the expectation of a boon given by the gatherer. The most potent such waters I've personally experienced came from dedicants of Athena, Apollo and Zeus at the Acropolis, Delphi and Olympia, respectively.

It is also possible to acquire water from a number of rivers sacred to Hellenic and Roman gods. Ask a priest of these gods for details of appropriate rites.

Iron-Infused Water

The simplest iron-infused water comes from springs with very high iron concentrations. In my experience, the bacteria of these springs makes the water less effective, so it's best to boil, then freeze, the iron water.

You can also make iron infused water by taking an old iron pot, scouring it with steel wool, then setting water to boil in it for a minimum of ten minutes. This is a relatively easy technique.

The most traditional, and most potent from the POV of fighting energy beings, is formed by pouring distilled deionized water through a hole drilled within a magnetic lodestone. Add a couple of measures of salt to the water after pouring and stopper inside an earthenware of iron flask and you've got a pretty strong disruptor for minor energy beings and boggles. Add a few tablespoons of magnetite powder to the mix and you've got something that will pretty much put a major hurt on every energy being out there. Hitting some boggles with a solution of salt, magnetite powder and pure water is like hitting a human with napalm. They won't bother you a second time, but I would not advise doing it to things of human or higher sentience, especially things that gather in clans and kingdoms. Even if it's not a natural resident of our world, it's not good to damage things which have kinsmen who will avenge them.

Gift of the Magi Incense

Burn this upon hot coals. It doesn't work well as a stick.

To twelve measures of powdered sandalwood, add one measure (by volume) of edible flake gold and thirteen measures each of frankincense and myrrh. Use a hand grinder until it is of a similar consistency, then place in a glass baking dish and bake at 400° for 5 minutes or until the resins melt. Allow to cool, then break into pieces.

Resources

The following resources should provide you with more than enough information to boggle and stun the civilians in your life. Some of the links are to information, others are to books. I leave you to sort out which are for show and which are for real magic.

Indigo Children:

http://www.selectsmart.com/twyman.html

http://www.usatoday.com/news/religion/2005-05-31-indigo-kids_x.htm

Little Emperors:

http://www.mercatornet.com/articles/only_child_sorry_no_job/

LBRP:

http://www.geocities.com/nu_isis/lbrp.html

http://www.asiya.org/lbrp.html

http://www.ritualmagick.org/Divine+Hebrew+Na

mes+Associated+with+the+LBRP

http://www.sacred-texts.com/bos/bos546.htm

http://www.theisticsatanism.com/rituals/standard/

banishing.html